Favorite Stories by

JOHN A. ROWE

· · · · · · · · · · · · ·

3 Complete Tales

Favorite Stories by

JOHN A. ROWE

· · · · · · · · · · · ·

3 Complete Tales

PETER PIGLET

BABY CROW

SMUDGE

SMITHMARK

This edition published in 1999 by SMITHMARK Publishers,
a division of U.S. Media Holdings, Inc.,
115 West 18th Street, New York, NY 10011; 212-519-1300.

SMITHMARK books are available for bulk purchase for sales promotion and premium use. For details write or call the manager of special sales, SMITHMARK Publishers, 115 West 18th Street, New York, NY 10011.

ISBN: 0-7651-1685-5

Library of Congress Cataloging-in-Publication Data

Rowe, John A.
        Favorite stories by John A. Rowe: 3 complete tales.
            p.   cm.
        Contents: Peter Piglet — Baby Crow — Smudge.
        ISBN: 0 7651 1685 5
        [1. Children's stories, English. 2. Animals Juvenile fiction.
    3. Short stories. 4. Animals Fiction.] I. Title.
    PZ7.R7939Fav 1999
    [Fic] — dc21   99-24800
                                                    CIP

Printed in Hong Kong

10 9 8 7 6 5 4 3 2 1

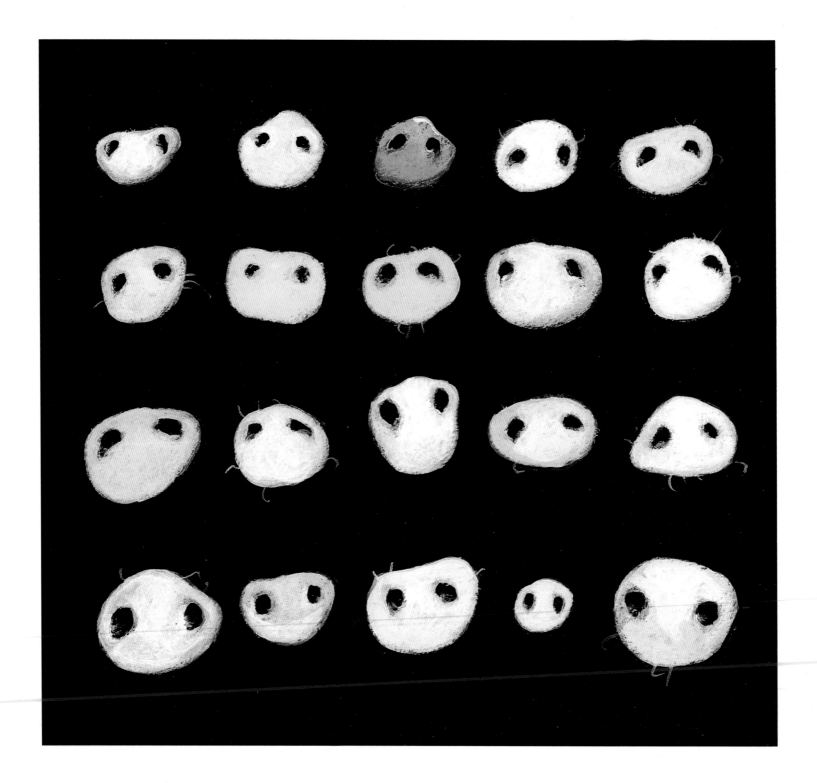

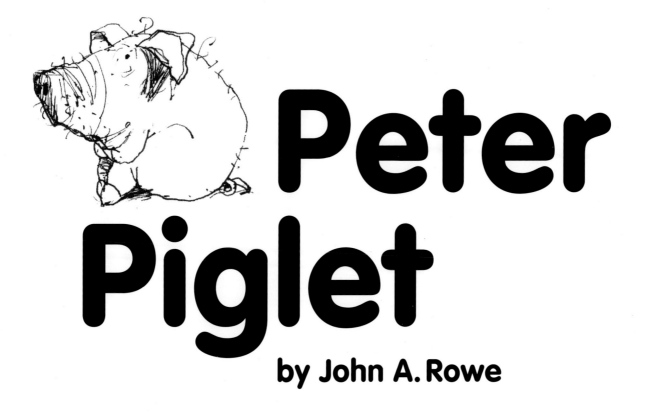

Peter Piglet

by John A. Rowe

Peter Piglet is a chubby fellow with no nose to speak of and a tail like a corkscrew. He is as soft as raspberries and as pink as a rose. He lives in the woods at the edge of my garden.

One morning while Peter snoozed beneath a warm summer sky, along came a gentle breeze filled with secret perfumes and the buzz of busy bees. The breeze tickled the hairs on his nose and woke him.

He rolled over among the yellow dandelions and stretched. It was a lovely day for a walk. So Peter Piglet trotted off through the woods that sunny morning, and he cast a big shadow beneath the mighty oaks.

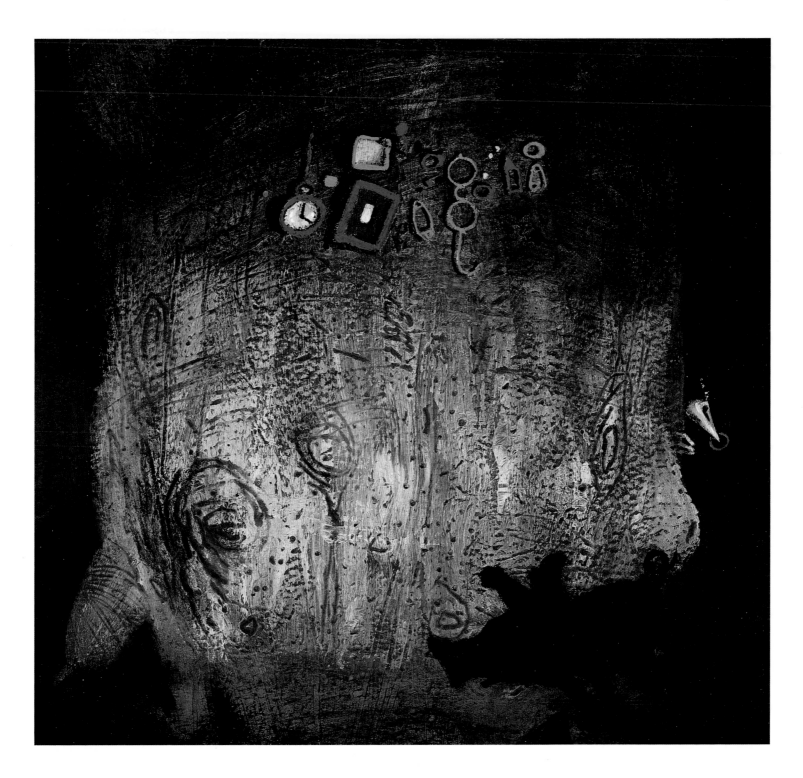

Before long he came upon a pile of sticks decorated with acorns and blackbird feathers. Being naturally curious, he stuck his nose right in and sniffed.

He could hardly believe what he found! There, lying neatly side by side, was a pair of beautiful golden shoes!

Peter sat back and scratched his head. He hardly dared to breathe in case it was all a dream. But dragonfly wings hummed in his ear—he was wide awake!

"Oh, how beautiful!" he whispered. Then, before Peter knew what had happened, he had slipped one foot in . . . then the other.

Clouds in the shapes of wonderful shoes drifted across the blue sky, and the skylarks sang dancing tunes. Peter Piglet was so happy.

Peter had never worn shoes before, and at first he found it very difficult to walk in them. But he kept trying until he became quite an expert.

And as he did, he grew to love those golden shoes more and more.

He went off to show the shoes to that pincushion on legs, Hedgehog.

"Oh, yes," agreed Hedgehog, "they do make you look rather nice indeed!"

"And look how well I can walk, too!" cried Peter proudly. And he proceeded to show Hedgehog a few fancy steps.

"Oh, yes," agreed Hedgehog, "you do walk rather well indeed!"

And so Peter Piglet spent the rest of the afternoon showing Hedgehog the finer points of walking, and dancing, and skipping, and hopping, and climbing, and even *swimming* in his golden shoes.

And in no time at all the Man in the Moon was looking down, and he bathed Peter with his shiny light.

Poor Peter was exhausted—and so were his feet! Placing the golden shoes by his head for safekeeping, he curled up among the foxgloves and ferns and fell into a deep sleep.

That night Peter Piglet dreamed of princes and swirling ballrooms, and his little pink legs danced and jiggled about—keeping time with some unknown, dreamy music. His snoring could be heard for miles. The early-morning dew fell silently and settled on Peter like powdered sugar on a marshmallow. Sleepy green caterpillars swayed ever so gently on silken threads as early birds dug for worms.

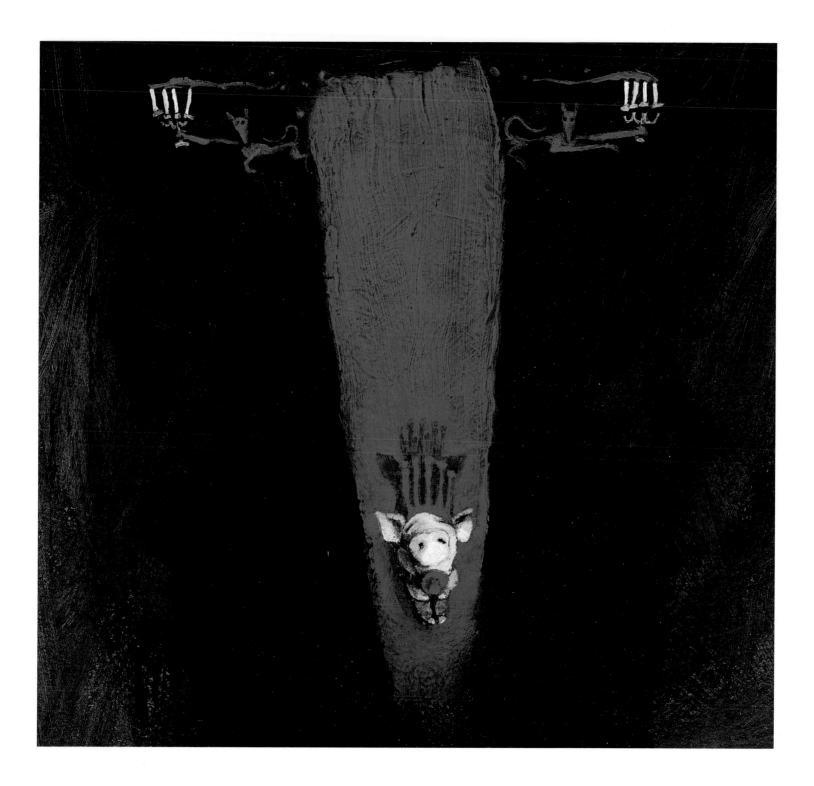

Peter Piglet awoke early, and a moment later he turned as white as a snowflake. His golden shoes were gone—vanished! What a shock!

Peter searched high and low. He climbed trees, stuck his head down rabbit holes, but he couldn't find those shoes anywhere. Peter asked Owl, that fine-feathered old hooter, if he had seen the shoes with his big eyes.

He asked Mole, that gentleman in the velvet waistcoat, if he had heard anything about the shoes with his sharp ears. He even asked Hedgehog, that old hairbrush with a nose, if he had smelled them. But nobody could help him.

Poor Peter Piglet was so sad. He looked down at his bare feet, and a big tear rolled down his wrinkly nose and fell to the ground with a loud plop.

He sat down on top of a hill and sighed deeply. Clouds in the shape of tears rolled across the gloomy sky while blackbirds called sadly to each other. Peter didn't know if he could live without those golden shoes.

His life had become ordinary.

Suddenly a tiny voice said, "Just look at my magnificent house!"

Peter jumped up in surprise and looked around, but he saw no one.

"No, down here!" called the tiny voice.

Peter looked down. "Why . . . that's one of my golden . . ."

"Isn't it wonderful!" said an old, wrinkly tortoise. "I had lost my house in a storm and I had nowhere to live. Then I found this beautiful golden palace—now I'm so happy!"

"B-b-but . . ." stuttered Peter Piglet.

"I know," said Tortoise with a smile. "It's only an old shoe, but it has saved my life, and now I couldn't be happier."

"Er . . . but . . ." said Peter. He just didn't know what to say.

"Well, good-bye, Peter Piglet," said Tortoise, and he disappeared into the ferns again.

"Well, I never!" said Peter. "A tortoise in a golden palace!"

Before Peter had even caught his breath, he heard another soft voice—"Look! Just look at my fabulous cradle!"

Peter spun around. He peered down into the ferns, but he couldn't see a soul. Then he looked up and—"Why . . . that's my other golden . . ."

"Isn't it wonderful?" said a shiny blackbird. "I lost my nest in a strong wind, and my children had nowhere to live. Then I found this beautiful golden cradle—now we're all so happy!"

"But . . . but . . ." sputtered Peter Piglet.

"I know," said Blackbird with a smile. "It's only an old shoe, but it has saved our lives and we couldn't be happier."

"Er . . . yes, but . . ." gasped Peter. "I . . . er . . . yes, that's wonderful, but . . ."

And suddenly Peter Piglet saw that it really *was* wonderful! Tortoise and Blackbird were both so happy, and Peter was happy for them.

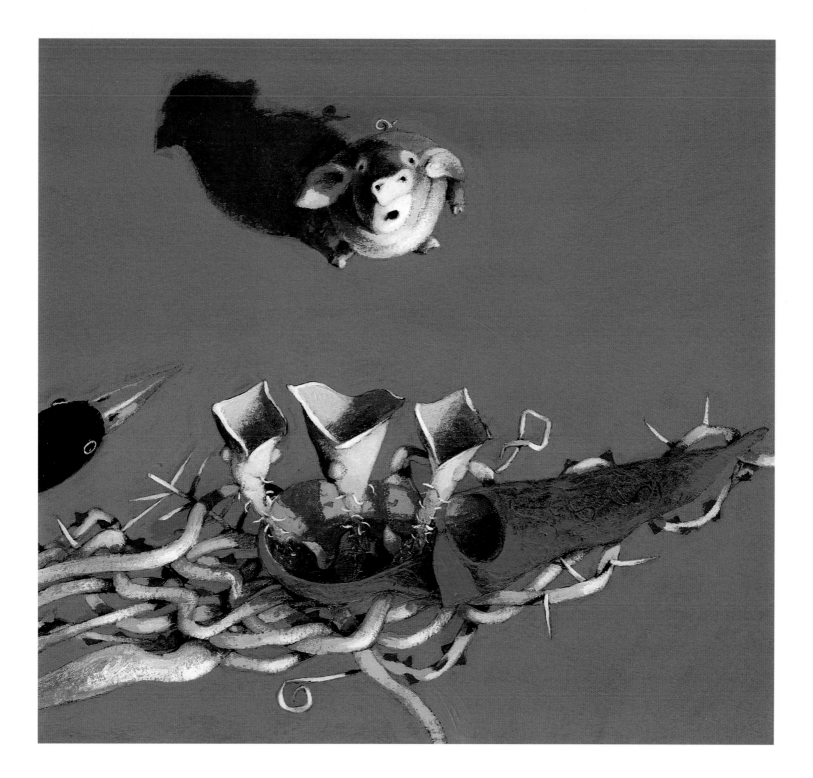

As Peter Piglet trotted off that sunny new day, he decided that life wasn't ordinary after all, and that for a little pig, it's much easier to walk without golden shoes!

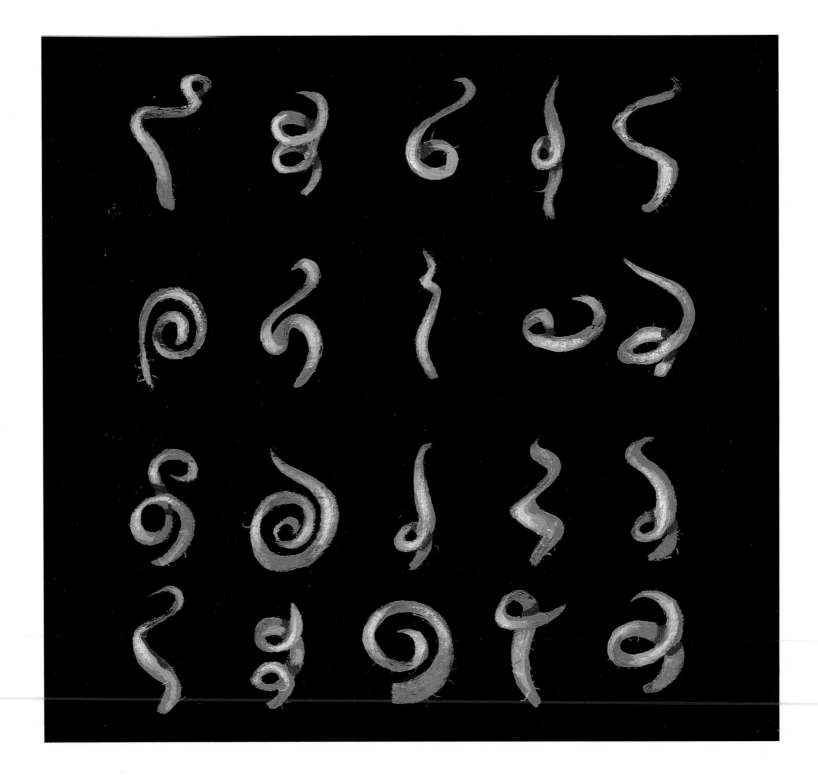

BABY CROW

JOHN A· ROWE

ONCE UPON A TIME, IN A TALL HOLLOW TREE, THERE LIVED A FLOCK OF CROWS. AT NIGHT THEY WOULD HANG THEIR HATS OUTSIDE THEIR ROOMS BEFORE THEY WENT TO SLEEP.

THE OLDEST CROWS LIVED AT THE TOP OF THE TREE. THE BRANCHES WERE THINNER UP THERE, WHICH MADE IT EASIER TO WEAR THEIR HATS. THEY SPENT MOST OF EACH DAY EITHER SLEEPING OR DISCUSSING THE PRICES OF NEW HATS.

GRANDFATHER CROW LIVED AT THE VERY TOP OF THE TREE. HE WAS OLD AND WISE. HE HAD LOST MANY OF THE FEATHERS IN HIS PLUMAGE, BUT HE STILL HAD HIS BEAUTIFUL VOICE.
IN HIS YOUTH, GRANDFATHER CROW HAD BEEN A FAMOUS OPERA SINGER. PEOPLE STILL CAME FROM FAR AWAY TO HEAR HIM SING.

OTHER TALENTED SINGERS LIVED TOWARDS THE BOTTOM OF THE TREE. THEY WOULD PROUDLY BELT OUT THEIR SONGS, AND THEY WORE THEIR AWARD MEDALS ON RIBBONS AROUND THEIR NECKS.

AND AT THE VERY BOTTOM OF THE TREE
LIVED BABY CROW. HIS FAMILY WAS PROUD
OF HIM, FOR THEY KNEW HE WAS GOING
TO BE A GREAT SINGER WHEN HE GREW UP.
BUT USUALLY BABY CROW JUST SAT IN
HIS NEST STARING OUT AT THE WORLD
AROUND HIM.

ONE DAY, WHEN FATHER CROW COULD WAIT NO LONGER, HE WENT TO BABY CROW AND SAID: "MY SON, IT'S TIME THAT YOU BEGAN TO SING. SAY KAAAAAW!"

"BEEP," SAID BABY CROW.

"NO...MUCH LOUDER," SAID FATHER CROW.

"BEEEEEEP," SAID BABY CROW, AS LOUDLY AS HE COULD.

FATHER CROW COULDN'T BELIEVE HIS EARS.

"MY BABY ISN'T A REAL CROW! HE CAN'T SING. WHAT SHALL I DO?" HE CRIED.

THAT MADE BABY CROW VERY SAD.
HE WANTED TO BE A REAL CROW.
SADLY HE HOPPED AWAY FROM THE TREE.
MOTHER CROW CALLED HIM BACK.
"LET ME TRY," SHE SAID. "NOW BABY CROW,
BREATHE DEEPLY, OPEN YOUR BEAK WIDE,
AND SING LIKE THIS...KAAAAAW!"
BABY CROW BREATHED IN...OPENED HIS
BEAK WIDE...AND SANG: "BEEEEEEP!"
FATHER CROW SHOOK HIS FEATHERS.
"WHAT SHOULD WE DO?" HE MOANED.
"TAKE HIM TO SEE GRANDFATHER CROW,"
SAID MOTHER CROW. "HE'LL KNOW WHAT
TO DO!"

"PLEASE HELP US, GRANDFATHER CROW,"
PLEADED FATHER CROW. "OUR BABY CAN'T
SING. ALL HE CAN SAY IS BEEP!"
"HMMM..." SAID GRANDFATHER CROW AS
HE SCRATCHED HIS HEAD. "LET ME THINK
A MOMENT." HE TURNED TO BABY CROW.
"SAY AAH."
"EEEEEP," SAID BABY CROW.
"HMMM..." SAID GRANDFATHER CROW.
"THIS IS MORE SERIOUS THAN I THOUGHT.
SAY DO-RE-ME."
"BEEEEEP...BEEEEEP...BEEEEEP," SAID BABY
CROW.

GRANDFATHER CROW GENTLY OPENED
BABY CROW'S BEAK WITH ONE CLAW.
"COUGH FOR ME, MY BOY."
BABY CROW DID AS HE WAS TOLD, AND
WHEN HE COUGHED, A LARGE RED CHERRY
THAT HAD BEEN STUCK IN HIS THROAT
FOR SOME TIME SHOT OUT AND HIT
GRANDFATHER CROW IN THE BEAK.
"OUCH!" SCREAMED GRANDFATHER CROW.
"LET THAT BE A LESSON TO YOU! CHEW YOUR
FOOD BEFORE YOU SWALLOW IT!"
"KAAAAAW!" SANG BABY CROW, SO LOUDLY
THAT EVERYONE LEAPT INTO THE AIR
WITH FRIGHT.
"MY SON!" CRIED FATHER CROW WITH
DELIGHT. "YOU CAN SING—SO LOUDLY!"

■

"KAAAAAW! KAAAAAW! KAAAAAW!" SANG BABY CROW AGAIN. HE WAS SO PLEASED TO BE A REAL CROW THAT HE WANTED THE WHOLE WORLD TO HEAR HIM.

"KAAAAAW! KAAAAAW! KAAAAAW!" ALL THROUGH THE NIGHT, WHILE THE OTHER CROWS TRIED THEIR BEST TO SLEEP, HE SANG AND SANG AND SANG.

"MY SON," SAID FATHER CROW WEARILY, "COULD YOU PERHAPS SING A LITTLE QUIETER?"

"KAAAAAW! KAAAAAW! KAAAAAW!" SANG BABY CROW LOUDER THAN EVER.

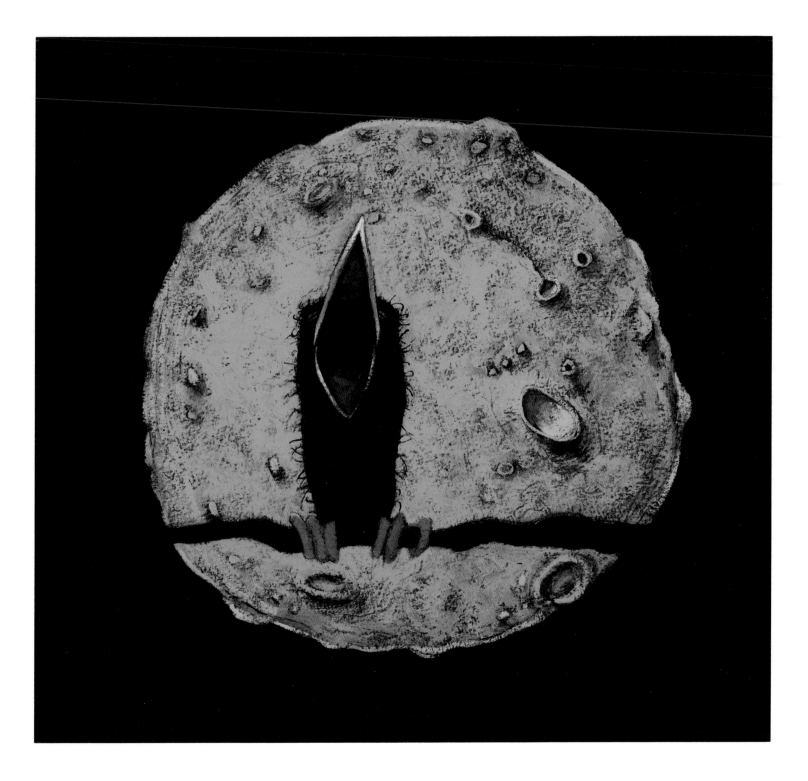

"OH DEAR," SAID MOTHER CROW, "I THINK I LIKED IT BETTER WHEN BABY CROW COULDN'T SING!"

"US TOO!" AGREED ALL THE OTHER CROWS IN THE TREE, PLUGGING THEIR EARS WITH CHERRIES.

"HE SANG 'BEEP' SO NICELY BEFORE!" SAID A TIRED CROW FROM THE NEXT TREE, WHO HADN'T SLEPT A WINK ALL NIGHT.

"I HAVE AN IDEA!" SAID FATHER CROW EXCITEDLY, AND HE FLEW OFF IN SEARCH OF THE CLOSEST CHERRY TREE.

"WOULD YOU LIKE A FEW CHERRIES?"
HE SAID TO THE TIRELESS SINGER WHEN HE
RETURNED.
"KAAAAAW! KAAAAAW! KAAAAAW!"
ANSWERED BABY CROW, GREEDILY
GOBBLING UP THE CHERRIES.
"WELL, HOW DO THEY TASTE?" ASKED
FATHER CROW.
BABY CROW ANSWERED: "BEEP!"
"WELL DONE!" SAID ALL THE OTHER CROWS.

"NOW BABY CROW CAN SING AS MUCH AS HE WANTS, AND WE'LL HAVE PEACE AND QUIET," SAID FATHER CROW.

THE FLOCK OF CROWS WAS CONVINCED THAT BABY CROW WOULD ONE DAY SING AS BEAUTIFULLY AS GRANDFATHER CROW, AND THAT PEOPLE WOULD COME FROM FAR AND WIDE TO HEAR HIM.

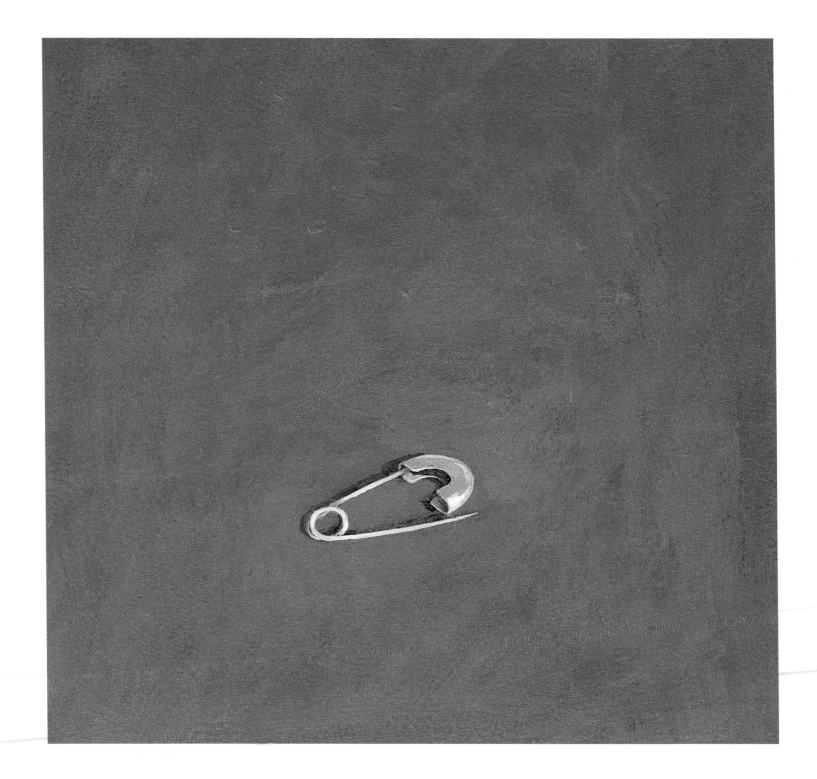

My name is Smudge, and I am black like burnt toast.

My whiskers are all tied in knots, and I sat in some chewing gum, but that doesn't matter.
I am old, and I tell stories.
And here's one now.

Long ago, before my tail became stiff like a broom handle, I was sitting in the garden drinking some warm milk that my mother had just given me.

The sunshine and the sweet smell of flowers wrapped themselves around me like a blanket. Nearby, a grasshopper sang a cradle song, and I was drowsy and happy and warm.

All of a sudden, a big bird with beady eyes swept down from the sky. Giving my ear a sharp pinch, he picked me up and flew away with me.

I hardly had time to wave good-bye to my brothers and sisters before we disappeared over the treetops.

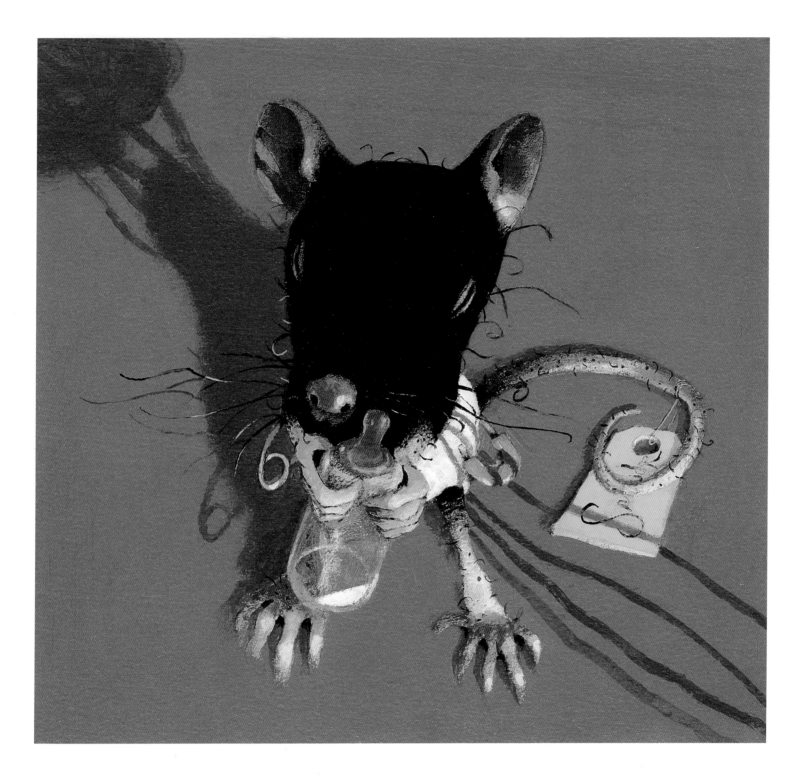

We soon reached the bird's home, which was filled with bald-headed babies.

At first they only used me as a brush to polish their long beaks. But as time passed, I grew quite close to them. Soon I felt just like one of the family.

I quickly learned to chirp and ruffle myself up. I even thought about laying an egg. But the one thing I just could not do—no matter how hard I flapped my arms—was fly like they could.

And one day, they all flew off without me. I hardly had time to wave good-bye to my new family before they disappeared behind a cloud.

I sat in the moist grass, wondering what to do next.

All of a sudden, a thin dog with a wet nose ran up. Giving my tail a quick bite, he picked me up and ran away with me.

We soon reached the dog's home, which was filled with growling babies.

At first they only used me as a ball to toss around. But as time passed, I grew quite close to them. Soon I felt just like one of the family.

I quickly learned to bark and wag my tail. I even thought about burying a bone. But the one thing that I just could not do—no matter how fast I moved my legs—was run like they could.

And one day they all ran off without me. I hardly had time to wave good-bye to my new family before they disappeared over a hill.

I sat on an old log and wondered what to do.

All of a sudden, a fluffy rabbit with big ears hopped out of hole. Giving my paw a hard squeeze, he picked me up and hopped away with me.

We soon reached the rabbit's home, which was filled with powder-puff babies.

At first they only used me to plug up a hole in the wall. But as time passed, I grew quite close to them. Soon I felt just like one of the family.

I quickly learned to nibble carrots and wiggle my ears. I even thought about digging a tunnel. But the one thing that I could not do—no matter how high I jumped—was hop like they could.

And one day they all hopped off without me. I hardly had time to wave good-bye to my new family before they disappeared in the tall grass.

I sat by a blue stream and wondered what to do.

All of a sudden, a long fish with silver scales swam up. Giving my toe a quick nibble, he pulled me down and swam away with me.

We soon reached the fish's home, which was filled with slippery babies.

At first they only used me as an anchor. But as time passed, I grew quite close to them. Soon I felt just like one of the family.

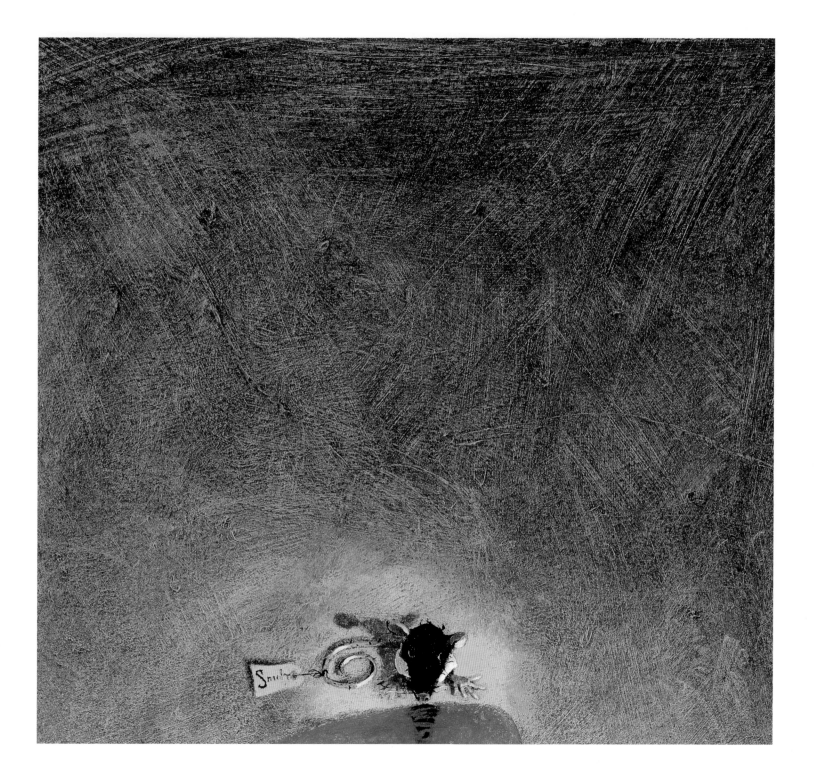

I quickly learned to hold my breath and blow bubbles. I even thought about making ripples. But the one thing I just could not do—no matter how quickly I flapped my feet—was swim like they could.

And one day they all swam off without me. I hardly had time to wave good-bye to my new family before they disappeared down the stream.

I sat beneath a shady tree and wondered what to do.

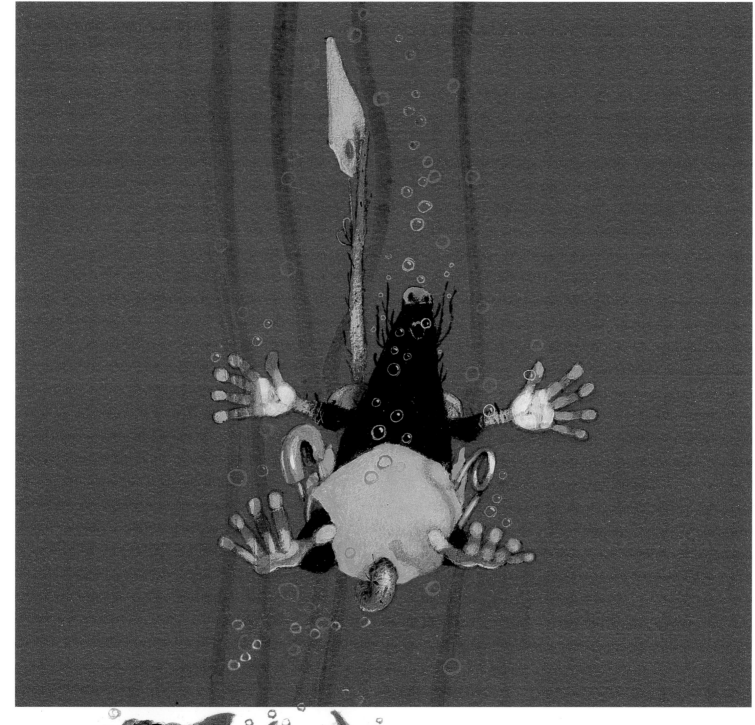

All of a sudden, a grey squirrel with a bushy tail climbed down. Giving my whiskers a brisk tug, he pulled me up and scampered away with me.

We soon reached the squirrel's home, which was filled with bushy-tailed babies.

At first they only used me as a pillow. But as time passed, I grew quite close to them. Soon I felt just like one of the family.

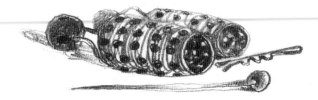

I quickly learned to hang upside down and balance on thin branches. I even thought about storing acorns. But the one thing that I just could not do—no matter how far I leaped—was jump like they could.

And one day they all jumped off without me. I hardly had time to wave good-bye to my new family before they disappeared through the leaves.

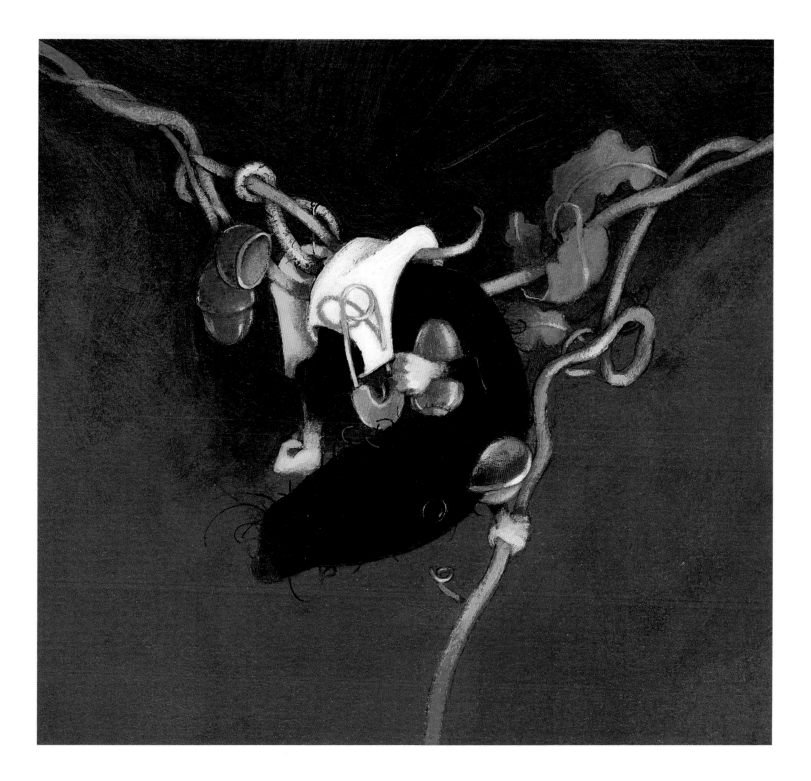

I sat in a garden and wondered what to do.

All of a sudden, a brown rat with a big smile was beside me. Giving my cheek a soft kiss, she cuddled me in her arms and carried me off.

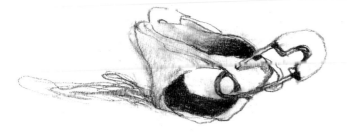

We soon reached the rat's nest, which was filled with long-tailed babies.

From the very first they didn't want to use me for anything—they just hugged and cuddled me and welcomed me home. Right away I felt close to them—just like one of the family, and of course I was, since they were my very own mother and brothers and sisters.

I already knew how to twitch my nose and squeak. I didn't even have to think about combing my whiskers. There wasn't a thing they could do that I couldn't do. For after all, I was a rat—just like them!

And I knew they would never leave me!

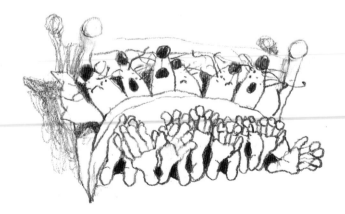